**PIANO
VOCAL
GUITAR**

"WILLY WONKA & THE CHOCOLATE FACTORY"

ISBN 978-0-634-03153-3

HAL•LEONARD®
CORPORATION
7777 W. BLUEMOUND RD. P.O. BOX 13819 MILWAUKEE, WI 53213

Visit Hal Leonard Online at
www.halleonard.com

CONTENTS

THE CANDY MAN

Words and Music by LESLIE BRICUSSE
and ANTHONY NEWLEY

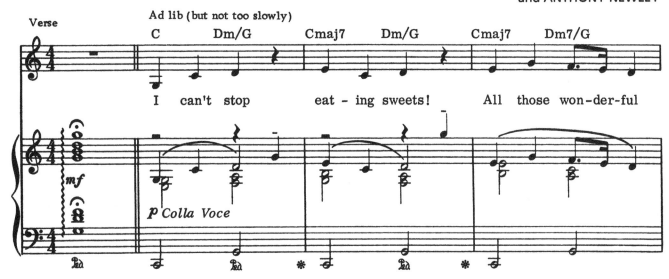

I can't stop eat-ing sweets! All those won-der-ful

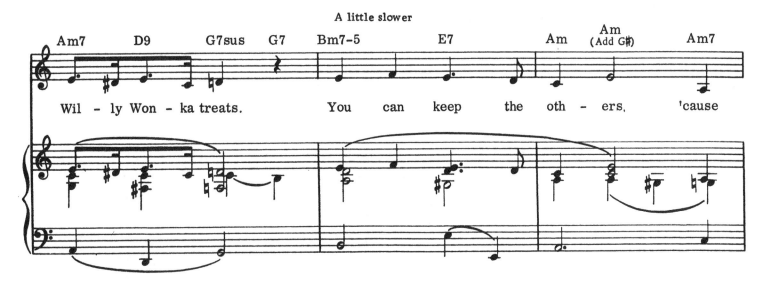

Wil-ly Won-ka treats. You can keep the oth-ers, 'cause

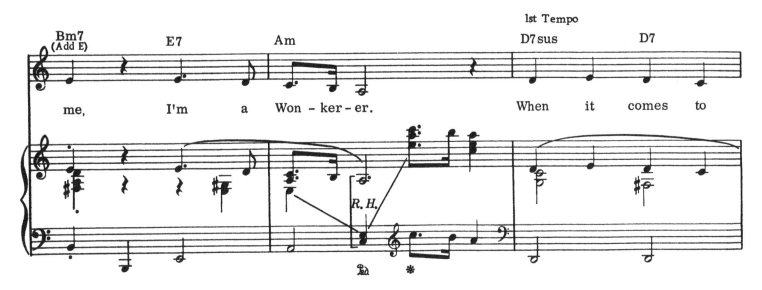

me, I'm a Won-ker-er. When it comes to

Refrain-Moderato, joyfully

Who can take a sun - rise____ sprin - kle it with dew,____
Who can take a rain - bow____ wrap it in a sigh,____

cov - er it in choc -'late and a mir - a - cle or two? The
soak it in the sun and make a straw-b'ry lem - on pie?

can - dy man,____ (The can - dy man,) the can - dy man can.____ (the

CHEER UP, CHARLIE

Words and Music by LESLIE BRICUSSE
and ANTHONY NEWLEY

Verse

You get blue like ev-'ry-one; But me and Grand-pa Joe_____ can

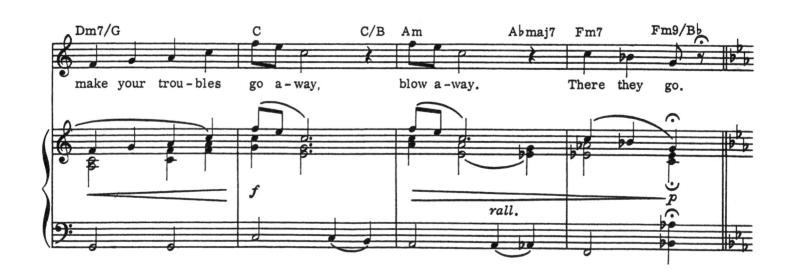

make your trou-bles go a-way, blow a-way. There they go.

Refrain

Moderately slow, Rubato and Tenderly

Cheer up, Char-lie,___ give me a smile. What hap-pened to the smile I used to

know? Don't you know your grin has al-ways been my sun-shine?

Let that sun-shine show!___ Come on, Char-lie,___

no need to frown. Deep down you know to-mor-row is your toy.

I WANT IT NOW

Words and Music by LESLIE BRICUSSE
and ANTHONY NEWLEY

OOMPA-LOOMPA DOOMPADEE-DOO

Words and Music by LESLIE BRICUSSE
and ANTHONY NEWLEY

Moderato

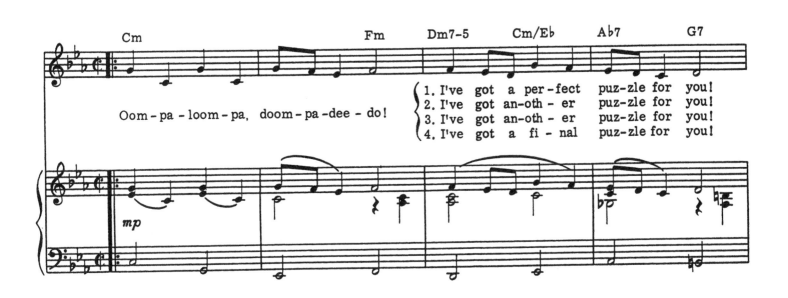

Oom-pa-loom-pa, doom-pa-dee-do!

1. I've got a per-fect puz-zle for you!
2. I've got an-oth-er puz-zle for you!
3. I've got an-oth-er puz-zle for you!
4. I've got a fi-nal puz-zle for you!

Cm   Fm   Dm7-5   Cm/Eb   Ab7   G7

Oom-pa-loom-pa, doom-pa-dee-dee! If you are wise you-'ll lis-ten to me!

Cm   Fm   Dm7-5   Cm/Eb   Ab7   G7   Cm

I'VE GOT A GOLDEN TICKET

Words and Music by LESLIE BRICUSSE
and ANTHONY NEWLEY

PURE IMAGINATION

Words and Music by LESLIE BRICUSSE
and ANTHONY NEWLEY

THE BEST EVER

COLLECTION
ARRANGED FOR PIANO, VOICE AND GUITAR

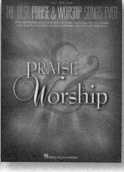

150 OF THE MOST BEAUTIFUL SONGS EVER
00360735 150 ballads.............................$32.99

BEST ACOUSTIC ROCK SONGS EVER
00310984 65 acouistic hits.....................$22.99

MORE OF THE BEST ACOUSTIC ROCK SONGS EVER
00311738 69 songs................................$19.95

BEST BIG BAND SONGS EVER
00286933 66 favorites $19.99

BEST BLUES SONGS EVER
00312874 73 blues tunes $19.99

BEST BROADWAY SONGS EVER - 6TH EDITION
00291992 85 songs................................$24.99

MORE OF THE BEST BROADWAY SONGS EVER
00311501 82 songs................................$22.95

BEST CHILDREN'S SONGS EVER
00159272 101 songs..............................$19.99

BEST CHRISTMAS SONGS EVER
00359130 69 holiday favorites...............$27.50

BEST CLASSIC ROCK SONGS EVER
00289313 64 hits...................................$24.99

THE BEST COUNTRY ROCK SONGS EVER
00118881 52 hits $19.99

THE BEST CONTEMPORARY CHRISTIAN SONGS EVER – 2ND EDITION
00311985..$21.99

BEST COUNTRY SONGS EVER
00359135 76 classic country hits...........$22.99

BEST DISCO SONGS EVER
00312565 50 songs................................$19.99

THE BEST DIXIELAND SONGS EVER
00312326..$19.99

BEST EARLY ROCK 'N' ROLL SONGS EVER
00310816 74 songs................................$19.95

BEST EASY LISTENING SONGS EVER
00359193 75 mellow favorites...............$22.99

BEST FOLK/POP SONGS EVER
00138299 66 hits $19.99

BEST GOSPEL SONGS EVER
00310503 80 gospel songs.....................$19.99

BEST HYMNS EVER
00310774 118 hymns $18.99

BEST JAZZ STANDARDS EVER
00311641 77 jazz hits............................$22.99

BEST LATIN SONGS EVER
00310355 67 songs................................$19.99

BEST LOVE SONGS EVER
00359198 62 favorite love songs...........$19.99

THE BEST MOVIE SONGS EVER SONGBOOK – 5TH EDITION
00291062 75 songs................................$24.99

BEST MOVIE SOUNDTRACK SONGS EVER
00146161 70 songs................................$19.99

BEST POP/ROCK SONGS EVER
00138279 50 classics $19.99

BEST PRAISE & WORSHIP SONGS EVER
00311057 80 all-time favorites...............$22.99

BEST R&B SONGS EVER
00310184 66 songs................................$19.95

BEST ROCK SONGS EVER
00490424 63 songs................................$18.95

BEST SONGS EVER
00265721 71 must-own classics............$24.99

BEST SOUL SONGS EVER
00311427 70 hits $19.95

BEST STANDARDS EVER, VOL. 1 (A-L)
00359231 72 beautiful ballads...............$17.95

BEST STANDARDS EVER, VOL. 2 (M-Z)
00359232 73 songs................................$17.99

MORE OF THE BEST STANDARDS EVER – VOL. 2 (M-Z) – 2ND EDITION
00310814..$17.95

BEST WEDDING SONGS EVER
00290985 70 songs................................$24.99

HAL•LEONARD®
Visit us online
for complete songlists at
www.halleonard.com

BIG BOOKS of Music

Arrangements for piano, voice, and guitar in books with stay-open binding, so the books lie flat without breaking the spine.

BIG BOOK OF BIG BAND HITS
84 songs: Alright, Okay, You Win • Caravan • Don't Get Around Much Anymore • I Can't Get Started with You • In the Mood • Old Devil Moon • Sentimental Journey • Star Dust • Stompin' at the Savoy • A String of Pearls • Take the "A" Train • Tuxedo Junction • more!
00310701 .... $22.99

BIG BOOK OF BLUEGRASS SONGS
70 songs: Alabama Jubilee • Blue Moon of Kentucky • Dark Holler • I Am a Man of Constant Sorrow • Mule Skinner Blues • Orange Blossom Special • Rocky Top • Wildwood Flower • and more.
00311484 .... $22.99

BIG BOOK OF BLUES
80 songs: Baby Please Don't Go • Caldonia • I'm a Man • Kansas City • Milk Cow Blues • Reconsider Baby • Wang Dang Doodle • You Shook Me • and scores more.
00311843 .... $19.99

BIG BOOK OF BROADWAY
70 songs: All I Ask of You (from *The Phantom of the Opera*) • Bali Ha'i (from *South Pacific*) • Bring Him Home (from *Les Misérables*) • Luck Be a Lady (from *Guys and Dolls*) • One (from *A Chorus Line*) • Seasons of Love (from *Rent*) • Singin' in the Rain • and more!
00311658 .... $22.99

BIG BOOK OF CHILDREN'S SONGS
55 songs: Camptown Races • (Oh, My Darling) Clementine • Do-Re-Mi • Eensy Weensy Spider • Hickory Dickory Dock • Humpty Dumpty • John Jacob Jingleheimer Schmidt • Mickey Mouse March • Pop Goes the Weasel • This Land Is Your Land • Yellow Submarine • more!
00359261 .... $17.99

BIG BOOK OF CHRISTMAS SONGS
126 songs: Away in a Manger • Carol of the Bells • Good King Wenceslas • It Came upon the Midnight Clear • Joy to the World • O Holy Night • The Twelve Days of Christmas • We Wish You a Merry Christmas • and more.
00311520 .... $22.99

BIG BOOK OF CONTEMPORARY CHRISTIAN FAVORITES
50 songs: Big House • Follow You • I Still Believe • Let Us Pray • More Beautiful You • People Need the Lord • Sing, Sing, Sing • Thy Word • What Are You Waiting For • You Reign • and many more.
00312067 .... $21.99

Prices, contents, and availability subject to change without notice.

BIG BOOK OF '50S & '60S SWINGING SONGS
67 songs: All the Way • Blame It on the Bossa Nova • Dream Lover • I Left My Heart in San Francisco • Love and Marriage • Moonglow • That's Amore • You Belong to Me • and more.
00310982 .... $19.95

BIG BOOK OF FOLKSONGS
125 songs: Cotton Eyed Joe • Down by the Salley Gardens • Frere Jacques (Are You Sleeping?) • Hatikvah • Mexican Hat Dance • Sakura • Simple Gifts • Song of the Volga Boatman • The Water Is Wide • and many more.
00312549 .... $24.99

BIG BOOK OF FRENCH SONGS
70 songs: April in Paris • Autumn Leaves • Beyond the Sea • Can Can • I Dreamed a Dream • La Marseillaise • My Man (Mon Homme) • Sand and Sea • Un Grand Amour (More, More & More) • Where Is Your Heart • and more.
00311154 .... $22.99

BIG BOOK OF GERMAN SONGS
78 songs: Ach, Du Lieber Augustin • Ave Maria • Bist Du Bei Mir • O Tannenbaum • Pizzicato Polka • Ständchen • Vilja Lied • and dozens more!
00311816 .... $19.99

BIG BOOK OF GOSPEL SONGS
100 songs: Amazing Grace • Because He Lives • Give Me That Old Time Religion • His Eye Is on the Sparrow • I Saw the Light • My Tribute • The Old Rugged Cross • Precious Lord, Take My Hand • There Is Power in the Blood • Will the Circle Be Unbroken • and more!
00310604 .... $19.95

BIG BOOK OF HYMNS
125 songs: Blessed Assurance • For the Beauty of the Earth • Holy, Holy, Holy • It Is Well with My Soul • Just As I Am • A Mighty Fortress Is Our God • The Old Rugged Cross • What a Friend We Have in Jesus • and more.
00310510 .... $22.99

BIG BOOK OF IRISH SONGS
75 songs: Danny Boy • The Irish Washerwoman • Jug of Punch • Molly Malone • My Wild Irish Rose • Peg O' My Heart • 'Tis the Last Rose of Summer • Too-Ra-Loo-Ra-Loo-Ra (That's an Irish Lullaby) • When Irish Eyes Are Smiling • and more.
00310981 .... $19.99

BIG BOOK OF ITALIAN FAVORITES
80 songs: Carnival of Venice • Funiculi Funicula • Italian National Anthem • La Donna É Mobile • Mambo Italiano • Mona Lisa • O Mio Babbino Caro • Speak Softly, Love • Tarantella • That's Amore • and more!
00311185 .... $19.99

BIG BOOK OF JAZZ
75 songs: Autumn Leaves • Days of Wine and Roses • Falling in Love with Love • Honeysuckle Rose • I've Got You Under My Skin • My One and Only Love • Satin Doll • Take the "A" Train • The Way You Look Tonight • and more.
00311557 .... $24.99

BIG BOOK OF LATIN AMERICAN SONGS
89 songs: Always in My Heart • Feelings (Dime?) • The Girl from Ipanema • Granada • It's Impossible • La Cucaracha • Malaguena • Manha de Carnaval (A Day in the Life of a Fool) • What a Diff'rence a Day Made • and more!
00311562 .... $22.99

BIG BOOK OF LOVE SONGS
82 songs: All of Me • Endless Love • (Everything I Do) I Do It for You • Just the Way You Are • My Heart Will Go On (Love Theme from 'Titanic') • The Power of Love • Thinking Out Loud • Unchained Melody • Wonderful Tonight • You Raise Me Up • and more.
00257807 .... $22.99

BIG BOOK OF MOTOWN
84 songs: Baby Love • Get Ready • I Heard It Through the Grapevine • Just My Imagination • Lady Marmalade • My Girl • Reach Out, I'll Be There • Shop Around • Three Times a Lady • You Are the Sunshine of My Life • and more.
00311061 .... $22.99

BIG BOOK OF MOVIE MUSIC
74 songs: Beauty and the Beast • City of Stars • Eye of the Tiger • How Far I'll Go • Theme from "Jaws" • Over the Rainbow • Singin' in the Rain • Skyfall • The Sound of Music • What a Wonderful World • and more.
00260523 .... $22.99

BIG BOOK OF NOSTALGIA
158 songs: After the Ball • The Bells of St. Mary's • The Darktown Strutters' Ball • A Good Man Is Hard to Find • I'm Always Chasing Rainbows • If I Had My Way • Oh! You Beautiful Doll • Pretty Baby • Swanee • You Made Me Love You (I Didn't Want to Do It) • and more.
00310004 .... $27.50

BIG BOOK OF OLDIES
73 songs: All My Loving • Barbara Ann • Crying • (Sittin' on) The Dock of the Bay • Good Vibrations • Great Balls of Fire • Kansas City • La Bamba • Mellow Yellow • Respect • Soul Man • Twist and Shout • Windy • and more.
00310756 .... $22.99

BIG BOOK OF PRAISE & WORSHIP
52 songs: Build Your Kingdom Here • Cornerstone • Forever Reign • Lord, I Need You • One Thing Remains (Your Love Never Fails) • 10,000 Reasons (Bless the Lord) • This Is Amazing Grace • Whom Shall I Fear • and more.
00140795 .... $24.99

BIG BOOK OF ROCK
78 songs: All Right Now • Born to Be Wild • Crocodile Rock • Dust in the Wind • Fly Like an Eagle • Free Bird • Jump • Livin' on a Prayer • Paradise City • Rock and Roll All Nite • Smoke on the Water • Walk This Way • Working for the Weekend • You Really Got Me • and more.
00241569 .... $22.99

BIG BOOK OF STANDARDS
86 songs: April In Paris • Beyond the Sea • Blue Skies • Cheek to Cheek • I Left My Heart In San Francisco • Isn't It Romantic? • It's Impossible • Ol' Man River • Out Of Nowhere • Puttin' on the Ritz • Star Dust • That Old Black Magic • The Way We Were • What Now My Love • and more.
00311667 .... $19.95

BIG BOOK OF SWING
84 songs: Air Mail Special • Boogie Woogie Bugle Boy • In the Mood • Jukebox Saturday Night • Mood Indigo • Stompin' at the Savoy • A String of Pearls • Take the "A" Train • That Old Black Magic • Tuxedo Junction • and more.
00310359 .... $19.95

BIG BOOK OF TORCH SONGS
75 songs: All Alone • Bewitched • Crazy • Good Morning Heartache • Here's That Rainy Day • In a Sentimental Mood • Misty • 'Round Midnight • Stormy Weather • Too Young • and more.
00310561 .... $19.99

BIG BOOK OF TV THEME SONGS
71 songs: The Big Bang Theory • Breaking Bad • Downton Abbey • Friends • Game of Thrones • I Love Lucy • Jeopardy • M*A*S*H • NFL on Fox • The Office • The Simpsons • The Sopranos • Star Trek® • and more.
00294317 .... $22.99

BIG BOOK OF WEDDING MUSIC
77 songs: Ave Maria • Canon in D • Endless Love • In My Life • Jesu, Joy of Man's Desiring • The Lord's Prayer • Trumpet Voluntary • We've Only Just Begun • Wedding March • Wedding Processional • You Are So Beautiful • and more.
00311567 .... $22.99

0121
294